Essays o

North America and the Beginnings of European Colonization

by Karen Ordahl Kupperman

Carla Rahn Phillips and
David J. Weber, Series Editors

American Historical Association
400 A Street S.E., Washington, D.C. 20003

KAREN ORDAHL KUPPERMAN is professor of history at the University of Connecticut and specializes in the colonization of America, its European background, and its effect on American natives and settlers. She currently chairs the Council of the Institute of Early American History and Culture, and served from 1989 to 1992 on the Board of Editors of the *William and Mary Quarterly*, which she also chaired in 1991-92. Dr. Kupperman has published four books: *Settling With the Indians: The Meeting of Indian and English Cultures in America, 1580-1640* (1980); *Roanoke: The Abandoned Colony* (1984); *Captain John Smith: A Select Edition of His Writings* (1988); and *Major Problems in American Colonial History* (1993). Currently in press with Cambridge University Press is *Providence Island, 1630-1641: The Other Puritan Colony*.

AHA Publications Editor: Roxanne Myers Spencer
Assistant Editor: Emily Frye
Staff Editor: Cecelia J. Dadian

Copyright © 1992 American Historical Association
All rights reserved. No part of this book may be reproduced in any form without permission in writing from the publisher, except by a reviewer who wishes to quote brief passages in connection with a review written for inclusion in a magazine or newspaper.

Published 1992 by the American Historical Association. As publisher, the American Historical Association does not adopt official views on any field of history and does not necessarily agree or disagree with the views expressed in this book.

ISBN: 0-87229-068-9

Library of Congress catalog card number: 92-074696
Printed in the United States of America

Contents

Foreword		v
Introduction		ix
I	Northern Experience	1
II	Southern Experience	5
III	The View at Mid-Century	9
IV	Santa Fe	15
V	Quebec	19
VI	Jamestown	25
VII	The Future of Colonization	29
Endnotes		35
Suggestions for Further Reading		40

Foreword

PROBING THE ISLANDS AND MAINLAND OF THE WESTERN HEMIsphere, Christopher Columbus and his contemporaries assumed initially that they had come to the edges of Asia. They did not, of course, suspect that other lands existed in the Western Hemisphere, but they knew much about the vast expanses and riches of the Orient, which they had sought by sailing westward across the Atlantic. After Columbus and dozens of other mariners had made that journey, many began to question their knowledge of geography: the lands and peoples they had happened upon differed markedly from the parts of Asia known to Marco Polo and other European travelers in the centuries before Columbus's voyage. The peoples who inhabited the Western Hemisphere experienced a similar shock of recognition. Their civilization had developed independently, and they had no more idea of the existence of Europe, Africa, or Asia than Europeans, Africans, or Asians had of them.

Columbus's first voyage began the irreversible process that brought those disparate groups of human beings into contact. Other voyages between Europe and the Western Hemisphere, and perhaps between Asia and the Western Hemisphere, had occurred before Columbus, but they had spawned no lasting contacts and no lasting consequences. In the wake of Columbus's first voyage, however, all of the great urban civilizations of the globe came into contact for the first time in human history. Those contacts persisted and grew with increasing intensity and complexity, eventually creating our interconnected and interdependent modern world.

Columbus's serendipitous arrival in what Spaniards mistakenly called the Indies in 1492 set into motion changes as profound as mankind can recall. As important as Columbus was to world history, however, he was not unique. He represented the combined knowledge, beliefs, and ambitions of Europeans developed over the previous thousand years. The 500th anniversary of Columbus's first voyage provides an ideal opportunity for historians to reflect on both the antecedents and the consequences of European exploration and trade. Only by understanding Columbus in his full European context can we begin to appreciate the meaning of his voyage. Similarly, only by understanding the historical context of the peoples of the Western Hemisphere can we appreciate the catastrophic effects of their contact with Europeans.

The American Historical Association's Committee for the Columbus Quincentennial has produced this pamphlet series as part of its commemoration of the 1992 anniversary. Of the many topics that pertain to the global encounter initiated by Columbus, we have selected several of especially broad interest. Each pamphlet focuses on a specific problem of historical interpretation, which teachers at the high school and college level may wish to discuss in their classrooms. To introduce these problems, we have chosen distinguished authors with broad historical sensibilities and deep understanding of aspects of the global encounter. In clear, brief essays, they explain and analyze the best recent evidence, and offer guidance to additional readings. Each pamphlet is, therefore, a convenient source for those of us who do not have time to study a question in depth, but who nonetheless want the most accurate information for our students.

In addition to the four pamphlets in this series, the American Historical Association publishes a series, *Essays on Global and Comparative History,* that examines exploration, trade, and migration over thousands of years of world history. In particular, we recommend the pamphlet in that series by Alfred W. Crosby, *The Columbian Voyages, the Columbian Exchange, and Their Historians* (Washington, D.C.: American Historical Association, 1987).

CARLA RAHN PHILLIPS DAVID J. WEBER
University of Minnesota *Southern Methodist University*
Series co-editors

Introduction

EUROPEAN COLONIZATION OF NORTH AMERICA WAS A HARD-WON achievement. Repeated Spanish, French, and English attempts to found permanent settlements were repelled; at times it almost seemed as if the land itself was actively hostile to European lifeways. Europeans were enormously proud of their new technological capacity and of the advances made by Renaissance art and science. Yet these confident venturers learned paradoxically that they had great difficulty in supporting themselves in a wide variety of environments where the American natives, whose cultures they deemed simple, lived well.

Again and again attempts to found settlements or "plantations" failed. Through hindsight we can see that settlers and planners defeated themselves by inadequate preparation for the rigors of transplantation, but these lessons were learned very slowly and at great human and monetary cost. Moreover, colonization of North America was retarded by lack of apparent incentives. Whereas the Caribbean and the South American mainland produced rich commodities, both agricultural and mineral, the huge continent to the north looked almost barren. The continent's huge bulk, standing as a barrier to contact with Asia, was disappointing to European colonial promoters in the first century after Columbus. Colonizing nations had shown strong initial interest in the land to the north. As early as the 1520s, France, Spain, and England all began searching the edges of the continent, questioning the natives they encountered for information about waterways systems and trade relationships linking the coast to the interior. In 1524, Giovanni da Verrazzano sailed for France and Estevão Gomes for Spain in voyages that extended from Newfoundland to Carolina. In 1527, John Rut made a similar voyage for England down the coast from Newfoundland. Although all three must have reported fully on their return to Europe, only Verrazzano's detailed account remains of these three early information-gathering attempts.

What these mariners sought was the waterway through the continent that logic told them must exist. Great entrances such as Chesapeake Bay with large rivers opening into it, Newport Harbor, and the Hudson River seemed to promise that the continent was not very broad (its east-west extent would not be known until much later) and that some system of waterways would allow passage for the small ocean-going ships of that time. When Verrazzano saw the sounds inside the North Carolina Outer Banks, he thought they were the South Sea, the Pacific Ocean. Because the mainland beyond them was flat and low-lying, he believed the water of the sounds stretched to the horizon. Thus these early voyages gave hope that the barrier presented by North America would be slight and easily overcome.[1]

Not only was this hope unrealistic, it also distorted Europe's early association with North America. Settlements continued to be conceived as bases to support traffic through the continent; the land was not seen as interesting in its own right. Promoters thus were little interested in developing genuine colonies—transplanted units of their home societies—and ensured that the relationship would be incidental to other, more immediately important goals. True colonization would not occur until promoters developed a clear set of aims based on realistic analysis of experience. This understanding would be won only by repeated failure.

I Northern Experience

THE HOPE OF AN EASY WATER ROUTE THROUGH THE CONTINENT gained strength in 1535, when French explorer Jacques Cartier reported on his trip up the greatest of the rivers that cut into the interior, the St. Lawrence. The previous year he had explored the coast and had brought to Europe two young men, Dom Agaya and Taignoagny, Iroquoians from Stadacona near where Quebec would later be built. By 1535 these men could speak French and guided Cartier into and up the St. Lawrence River. The explorers were excited by what they saw, especially when they reached the huge city of Hochelaga, near present-day Montreal. From the top of Mount Royal, they saw the river extending far into the interior, and the Indians told them that it intersected with other great waterways. The natives spoke of the Ottawa River and the Great Lakes, but Cartier and his backers in Europe were sure that the system of waterways must lead to the Pacific Ocean. He and his men had picked up stories of a rich nation far to the west, the Kingdom of Saguenay, whose people wore tailored clothing as the explorers did. Surely these stories referred to the wealthy nations of Asia. Europe buzzed with rumors after Cartier's return.[1]

Easy assumptions based on confusing information set promoters up for bitter failure when their hopeful conclusions were put to the test. Cartier's unprepared men suffered miserably through their first Canadian winter. We now know that the entire northern hemisphere was colder in the sixteenth and seventeenth centuries than it is today. Historical climatologists set this period apart as the Little Ice Age. Rivers throughout Europe that are today ice-free froze solid in the worst winters. The Canadian winter of 1535-36 was truly terrible.[2] Cartier wrote that the river was frozen to the depth of four fathoms, holding their ships fast, while on land the snow was four feet deep from mid-November to mid-April.

The unprepared French soon began to show symptoms of severe scurvy, with racking pains in their black and swollen arms and legs and rotting gums that caused their teeth to fall out. Fewer than ten of the 110 men were able-bodied by February; twenty-five died. The little colony was saved by Dom Agaya, who showed them how to gather and prepare a medicine from the foliage and bark of a tree they called Annedda, probably the Eastern White Cedar. The cure wrought by the vitamin C in the preparation was nothing short of miraculous, but that winter's experience meant Europeans were beginning to understand that colonization of North America would not be easily accomplished.[3]

Nonetheless the great St. Lawrence River's promise lured French explorers back. Cartier returned in 1541; his little fleet was the spearhead of a large attempt to found a colony under the overall command of a Protestant nobleman, Jean François de la Roque, Sieur de Roberval, and to follow up his leads to the promised passage to the Pacific. Cartier found only discouragement in his attempts to travel to the land of Saguenay; the many rapids along the St. Lawrence made travel in European vessels impossible. He also became convinced that the Indians would not welcome a permanent European presence. Roberval, who arrived a few months later, would not be dissuaded despite Cartier's fears and his own inadequate food supplies; his colony, the first to include women, suffered through a winter experience far worse than Cartier's. A quarter of the two hundred settlers died from scurvy and the others could be kept going only by the most heavy punishments. When the survivors returned to France, no one spoke of colonization again.[4] An English voyage under Captain Richard Hore in the mid-1530s had also met disaster; some of the men had allegedly been reduced to cannibalism to survive. Those who made it back to England told of "Mightie Islands of yce in the sommer season."[5] North America seemed distinctly unpromising; prospects for colonization were bleak and the passage through the continent, discovery and control of which alone could justify the expense and effort required by colonies, far longer and more difficult that they had hoped.

Northern North America was not abandoned by Europeans; promoters merely became more sophisticated in their approach. Rather than looking for uncertain rewards, mariners focused on the sure source of riches that had been known from the beginning of contact: the plentiful fishing off the Newfoundland Banks. Europe was experiencing a population explosion in the sixteenth and seventeenth centuries; the population doubled and accompanying inflation caused distress among the poor. Mariners were quick to exploit this plentiful new source of protein, North American fish.

Fishing called for a completely different relationship to America than colonization and exploration did. For one thing the fishing ships came in the spring and left in the fall, having preserved their fish by some combination of drying in the sun and layering them with salt in the ship's hold. The huge expense and commitment of colonies were unnecessary, and Europeans need only live through the relatively pleasant summer season. Moreover, anyone with a ship could take part. Whereas colonies required heavy investment up front and necessitated putting together corporate backing, fishing voyages required little prepayment of cash.[6]

Ironically as the official attitude of European governments and promoters was turning against exploitation of the North because of the dismal experiences of colonies, Newfoundland fishing was becoming established as a major industry by private merchants. As many as five hundred ships came to the Banks each year from all over Europe; French, Portuguese, Spanish, and English mariners worked in relative peace and amity to exploit this apparently inexhaustible wealth. The international community had worked out a system of self-government for their summer endeavors and elected an admiral each spring to lead them. The entanglements and expense of northern colonies were unnecessary.

II Southern Experience

WHILE FRANCE HAD TAKEN THE LEAD IN INVESTIGATING NORTHERN North America, Spanish explorers performed remarkable feats of reconnaissance in the South. Florida first attracted attention as an extension from Spain's thriving colonies in the Caribbean. Juan Ponce de León and Lucas Vásquez de Ayllón both tried to establish colonies there and northward to the Carolinas in the 1520s. The deaths of both commanders, combined with inadequate planning and native resistance to permanent settlement, frustrated these attempts. A third large Florida expedition under Pánfilo de Narváez simply disappeared altogether.

But these and other explorers left a legacy in their reports that the interior of the American Southeast was capable of producing rich commodities, and that inland Indians, like the Mayas and Aztecs farther south, lived in highly organized polities with quantities of precious minerals. Promoters easily assumed that ventures into the Southeast would repeat Spanish experience farther south, where Columbus and his successors originally encountered natives who lived quite simply, but met ever more sophisticated and wealthy societies as they moved west. Early leads were followed up by

Hernando de Soto, a man who had won fifteen years' experience and a personal fortune in the conquest of Central America and Peru. Soto organized an enormous expedition of seven hundred men and women, free and slaves, in 1537. His planning was strengthened by the sudden appearance in Mexico of four survivors from the 1528 Narváez expedition led by Alvar Nuãez Cabeza de Vaca, who had traveled across the entire southern portion of the continent on foot. These men had lived with natives on the Texas coast and had functioned as shamans. Thus Soto had access to genuine information about the interior.

Soto's huge company, with its two hundred horses and three hundred pigs, traveled throughout the entire Southeast, creating resentment wherever it went. All European powers put initial efforts at colonization into the hands of experienced military men. In their eyes, such a policy made sense because they believed security was the most fundamental concern. What they did not realize, and learned very slowly through experience, was that no European force, dependent as they all were on Indians for food, could ever be strong enough to be really secure in the face of sustained native hostility. And military expeditions always created hostility. Soto's policy was to ensure Indian cooperation by taking hostages wherever he and his men went. When the expedition was safely delivered to the next destination, new hostages were seized and the previous ones released. As long as they kept going, this plan functioned adequately, but later colonists would reap the consequences of this introduction to Europeans.

Soto took a circuitous route after landing in Florida in 1539, traveling northward to the Tennessee River, then south again almost to the Gulf, then again north across the Mississippi to the Arkansas River. On his way he visited members of the great Indian confederations of the Southeast, including Cofitachequi (near modern Augusta, Georgia), a Lower Creek tribe led by a female chief who offered him pearls, a presage of the rich gems and minerals they hoped to find. Soto and his men saw the descendants and constructions of the great Mound Builders at Coosa, the principal Upper Creek town (in modern Talladega County, Alabama). The explorers were moving toward the center of the great Mississippian Indian culture, and were impressed by the agricultural abundance and level of social organization they witnessed. They also encountered ever-greater resistance to the soldiers' strong-arm tactics; the expedition lost men and supplies in battles and raids. Soto himself died of fever in 1542 and the 311 remaining Spaniards returned to Mexico in 1543. Thus this expedition spanned the same period as the Cartier-Roberval venture in the North.[1]

Cabeza de Vaca's intelligence of his travels from Florida to Mexico between 1528 and 1537 inspired another roughly simultaneous Spanish venture—Francisco Vázquez de Coronado's expedition through the Southwest. Stories of the Pueblos, with their sophisticated city structures and intensive agriculture, became linked in promoters' minds with legends of fabulously wealthy provinces known as the Seven Cities of Cíbola, where the houses were lavishly decorated with turquoise and gold. The Spanish government, concerned about past treatment of American natives, was determined to inaugurate a new approach with this venture. The party was financed by heavy private investment, including funds from Coronado and many of his men; they were enjoined to carry all they would need and were forbidden to live off the land. Nor could they require Indians to work for them. The entire venture was predicated on the assumption that their finds in the North would replicate the riches discovered by earlier conquistadors.

The large expedition set out early in 1540 and soon hit rough going, as it moved into the arid lands of Arizona. When the advance party reached the main city of Cíbola, the Zuñi pueblo of Hawíkuh, the men were bitterly disappointed. Coronado recorded his reaction: "It is a small rocky pueblo, all crumpled up, there being many farm settlements in New Spain that look better from afar."[2] Like Soto's force, Coronado's met increasing native resistance to demands that the Indians acknowledge the overlordship of the Spanish king. After an Indian raid, the soldiers took Hawíkuh by force. Following a series of peaceful gestures, the natives who had fled returned to their pueblo and Coronado believed they had accepted the Spanish king and God. We can only guess what the Pueblos thought had occurred. The Indians' gifts of skins and turquoise that sealed the relationship were distinctly disappointing for soldiers who had expected riches beyond counting.

This pattern was reprised among the Hopis and at other pueblos, as smaller parties were sent out to investigate. One company of only twenty soldiers visited the Rio Grande pueblos, guided by a young man from Pecos Pueblo whom the Spaniards named Bigotes. Far less threatening than the large force, this small group was welcomed and entertained at Acoma, Taos, and Pecos. The soldiers erected a cross at each pueblo, and were pleased to see that the Indians decorated them with feathers and flowers, and placed sacred cornmeal before them just as they did their own altars. But even this small beginning was thrown away; conflict erupted when the soldiers thought Bigotes had found and concealed a gold bracelet. The soldiers attempted to force him to give it up. These men, like their backers, chose to participate in expeditions because they hoped to make their fortunes by whatever they could pick up. Treasure, once sighted, would not be relinquished.

These repeated incidents demonstrate the irresistible logic of expeditionary ventures composed of soldiers. Whatever their stated intentions, and regardless of how carefully they attempted to carry them out, the goal of replacing one rule by another, and especially of attempting to change the Indians' religious life, would always lead to conflict. Strategy was based on the fatal assumption that American natives would easily and willingly give up their own culture in preference for Roman Catholicism and a Spanish style of life. Native courtesy was mistaken for acquiescence, and the seeds of discord were sown. Later, when Indians made clear their determination to protect their own traditions, Europeans would perceive resistance as treachery. Soldier-colonists were always quick to react with force.

Coronado's main force traveled up into the Great Plains, in part looking for the great woolly cattle (buffalo) of which the Indians had told them. They camped on the Arkansas River. Ironically, Soto and Coronado were probably less than three hundred miles apart in their camps, but each was unaware of the other's presence. Because the two had taken such circuitous routes the ventures provided no precise evidence on the continent's east-west expanse. Wishful thinking and underestimating the extent of the land prevailed.

III The View at Mid-Century

BY THE MIDDLE OF THE SIXTEENTH CENTURY, EUROPEAN PROMOTERS knew a great deal about the shape and difficulties of North America, but what they knew was discouraging. North America did have much to offer in the way of fish, but other commodities were either nonexistent or would require a huge investment of money and lives to acquire or develop. In short, there was little encouragement for colonization; Spain turned back to its southern colonies, and European nations shared the Newfoundland fishing grounds. The vast continent of North America in between was left as useless.

There were others, however, who began to create an alternative vision of the promise of North America. Religious minorities, seeking refuge from persecution at home, saw that the qualities making the continent unattractive for development might enhance its appeal as a place where they could be left alone. French Protestants, Huguenots, first sought to settle on these terms as their country was rent by renewed sectarian violence. Warned by Cartier's experiences in the North, they looked south. In 1562 and 1564 parties led by Jean Ribault and by René Goulaine de Laudonnière attempted to plant along the East Coast, first Charlesfort on Port Royal Sound in South Carolina and then La Caroline on the St. John's River in Florida.

These tiny colonies learned some harsh lessons that others would relearn through bitter experience. No settlement, even one composed of families that intended to grow their own food, would succeed unless it could find a secure source of income. Mere survival was not enough; all American colonies continued to be dependent on Europe for supplies, and the process of peopling and supplying them was unbelievably expensive. Settlers, whatever their underlying goals, had to turn their efforts immediately to the search for wealth. Laudonnière wrote of "great store of Mulberrie trees white and red, on the toppes whereof there was an infinitive number of silke-wormes." He also passed on Indian lore of copper mines in the Appalachians, which he thought actually contained gold.[1]

Moreover, all early settlements were composed of mixed companies. Even those founded on religious grounds needed experts in war, weaponry, and the sea. Such men proved extremely difficult to control in the colonial setting, and their role exposed the basic conflict in thinking about colonization. Were colonies to replicate European society in America? Were they to be bases for military or economic activities? Would people come to stay permanently or would they rotate home after a time? Until these various questions were sorted out, the plantations would suffer from a sort of schizophrenia, attempting to act out many different, and conflicting, roles.

The Huguenot parties included women and children, indicating that they sought to build a new version of French society in America. But the realities of colonization, the constant need to pay for supplies and new settlers, meant that the colonists spent time looking for precious minerals. Some of La Caroline's young men, frustrated by their failure to find a rich commodity and the difficulties of exploring the mainland's rivers with clumsy European boats, seized a ship and went on an unauthorized privateering voyage. This sealed the fate of the colony.

Privateering—licensed piracy—was a common part of sixteenth-century maritime life. Nations authorized it as a way of harming their enemies, carrying on wars royal incomes were inadequate to support. Privateering was theoretically based on the principle of restitution. Merchants who had lost cargoes to enemy attacks applied to their own governments for licenses, called letters of marque or reprisal, to recoup their losses from ships belonging to merchants of the attacking nation. In theory they would stop as soon as they had recovered their deficit, but in fact a privateer, once licensed, could go on indefinitely. Most ships could be refitted as privateers, so little was required to join in. It was a high-stakes game. A single great prize could set investors up for life, but privateering was carried on with few restraints. Mariners received no wages and served for a share of the take, so they could become reckless.[2]

The most attractive magnet for privateers was the Florida channel. Sailing ships exiting the Caribbean must round the western end of Cuba and come up through one of two channels at the southern tip of Florida. All the wealth produced in the Spanish colonies, minerals as well as products such as the rich red dye cochineal, were collected in Havana and then were convoyed annually in a single large fleet to Seville. The privateers' dream was to detach one of the great carracks carrying American treasure.

The Spanish were determined to make such attacks as difficult as possible. They resolutely opposed any bases along the southern North American coast from which privateers could dash out to raid their shipping. Spanish authorities decided not only to eliminate the Huguenot base at La Caroline, but to create a fort of their own to forestall future aggression. Thus in 1565 a force led by Pedro Menéndez de Avilés wiped out the colonists he described as members of "the wicked Lutheran sect"; French sources wrote of a "terrible slaughter," a "massacre."[3]

Now, despite the low esteem in which earlier Spanish accounts held the mainland coast, Menéndez built a fort named San Agustín (St. Augustine) near the site of La Caroline. Not only was this fort necessary to protect the treasure fleet, but Menéndez and his advisors believed that Mexico lay a short way over the mountains to the west, and therefore San Agustín could also forestall future colonies that might attack New Spain. So the confused geographical picture begun by Verrazzano and bolstered by the reports of

Coronado, Cabeza de Vaca, and Soto fed the desire for North American colonies. Soon Menéndez also built a small fort, Santa Elena, on Parris Island in Port Royal Sound. These settlements were seen as preliminary to a major colonial effort. Spanish attention was drawn repeatedly to Chesapeake Bay, which they called the Bahía de Santa María de Ajácan. Numerous Spanish expeditions, including one led by Menéndez himself in 1561, had visited the great bay. Menéndez had captured a young Indian man, renamed Don Luis, who had provided information about the region. Many believed the large rivers emptying into the bay would ultimately reveal the long-sought waterway to the Pacific, and because only Spain had a presence in the West, it was in their interest to control access. Reports seemed to presage rich commodities and great Indian empires analogous to those Spanish explorers had found in Central and South America.

In 1570 Menéndez attempted to extend his settlements to the Chesapeake. This new colony was most unusual. It was composed entirely of Jesuit missionaries, except for Don Luis and a boy, Alonso de Olmos. Don Luis, who had lived in Spain and in Mexico and was a Roman Catholic convert, was expected to be the Jesuits' advocate in building strong ties. As advertisement of their intentions, the missionaries refused to take any soldiers with them. Their hopes misled them. Don Luis immediately rejoined his own people, and during the winter all the Jesuits were killed. Alonso de Olmos lived to tell their story. In sparing his life the Indians were communicating forcefully that, while they might welcome trade, they would not tolerate attempts to tamper with their own culture. Alonso represented the only form of contact they would allow.[4]

France and Spain, therefore, found only profound discouragement in their attempts to expand into southeastern North America. San Agustín was maintained and survives today as the oldest continuously occupied European settlement in North America, but plans to expand northward were given up, and Spain focused on its established colonies. As civil war raged in France, no further attempts to plant settlements emerged. North America's discouraging reputation was reinforced.

Nonetheless diverse interests conspired to force European nations to continue their involvement in North America. Faltering efforts through the later sixteenth century finally led to the creation of three small settlements within a few years of each other: Santa Fe by the Spanish in the Southwest in 1610; Jamestown by the English in the Southeast in 1607; and Quebec by the French in 1608. Where so much failure had preceded them, there was little reason to hope that these tiny tentative plantations would succeed, but they did hold on. Combined with the earliest colony, Spanish San Agustín in Florida, they provided the platform for the evolution of great colonial empires in the ensuing century and a half, and forever changed the native cultures they sought to displace and control.

IV Santa Fe

IN THE LATER SIXTEENTH CENTURY, SPANISH COLONISTS MADE MANY forays into the New Mexican territory; mostly these were unrecorded ventures by men running mining operations in northern Mexico. Two small exploring parties, both of which included missionaries, ventured north in the early 1580s. One was led by Fray Agustín Rodríguez and Captain Francisco Sánchez Chamuscado. The other was under Antonio de Espejo. These expeditions demonstrated that the Pueblos had not forgotten the lessons of the Coronado campaign, but the Spaniards largely had. Though they faced hardships, the returning explorers praised the land and its potential wealth and urged colonization. The friars among them stressed Spanish responsibility for converting the natives to Roman Catholicism, a process begun by now-martyred priests who had volunteered to stay in the North. These considerations led the Spanish government to decide on formation of a permanent colony in New Mexico.

Government machinery moved slowly. It was not until 1598 that Juan de Oñate, a creole (a person of European ancestry born in the colonies), led the first true colonial venture into the New Mexican territory; meanwhile slaving expeditions made repeated forays north. The colony's beginnings were inauspicious. Years of delay had cut into the company's supplies, and it had attracted too many men of checkered backgrounds. When they moved north into New Mexico, the Spanish declined to build their own settlement. Instead, they asked and received Indian permission to occupy two pueblos at the confluence of the Rio Grande and the Chama rivers, first San Juan (Ohke) and then San Gabriel (Yunque). Oñate moved through the region holding a series of great councils with Pueblo leaders and, he believed, received their acceptance both of Spanish rule and of Christianity. Although we cannot know what the Indians made of his explanation of the Christian worldview, we do know that the Pueblos did not have a system in which one ruler could speak for all. Each village was an independent unit, and even within the village decisions were made through consensus. The men who gathered to hear Oñate could make no promises for the Pueblos even if they understood what was being asked. Their subsequent actions demonstrate that the natives had no desire to replace their own cosmology and culture.

Nor did Spanish culture look impressive as manifested in Oñate's company. The newcomers were incapable either of housing or feeding themselves and expected to live off the Indians. In all colonial attempts, such dependence led to conflict. As Oñate's settlers had arrived too late to plant crops, they began to press Indian villages for food and firewood. A battle erupted between the residents of Acoma Pueblo and a small company of Spaniards in which the pueblo was almost completely destroyed. The aftermath illustrates the problems inherent in the cross-cultural experiment of colonization. Each culture interpreted events in terms of its own system and attempted to deal with unprecedented challenges in traditional ways.

Oñate held a trial replete with the most precise application of Spanish justice to determine who had been at fault at Acoma. The Native Americans were represented by the ablest man among the colonists. The story the court heard was very confused, but centered on one soldier's attempt to steal a turkey on a day when the soldiers were forcing the Indians to part with their corn. Turkeys were sacred birds to the Pueblos and were never eaten. Their feathers had key spiritual and economic significance. From the Indians' point of view the crime was comparable to a native taking a crucifix for a profane purpose, and was compounded by soldiers' demands for supplies backed up by force. Nonetheless, the court found the natives guilty of treason and all the Acoma men over twenty-five were sentenced to twenty years' servitude and to have one foot cut off. Women and children were also sentenced to servitude. Since a Spaniard convicted of the same crime would have been put to death, Oñate could see his judgment as lenient, and the trial as an example of scrupulous European justice. The Indians must have seen nothing but the most barbaric act of vengeance. Later, back in Mexico, Oñate himself stood trial for maltreatment of the natives, especially of the Acoma survivors, and suffered heavy penalties. We cannot doubt Spanish officialdom's sincere concern about the fate of the Indians within their own conception of justice. But the Indians, with a wholly different set of relationships, must have perceived this new force in their world as vicious.

Rivalry between religious and military authorities for control accentuated apparent Spanish unpredictability. In these early years of colonization, the greatest problem was control of the settlers, who found the reality of New Mexico cruelly disappointing in contrast to the reports that had attracted them. Oñate took a company northeast to the plains as far as modern Kansas during the summer of 1601. In his absence the colonists saw their crops wither in drought conditions, so they left for Mexico in October, before Oñate's return. Once again Spanish authorities concluded that the land to the North was not worth the effort needed to colonize it. But the priests accompanying Oñate had baptized many Indians; the crown now had the responsibility not to desert these souls. A few colonists held on with Oñate while officials decided what to do.

In 1608 the Viceroy of New Spain, Luis de Velasco, decided to continue the Spanish presence in New Mexico but not to allow adventurers such as Oñate to attempt to develop it. Fifty married soldiers would occupy a permanent settlement, and twelve friars would minister to them and the Christian Indians. No further expansion would be envisioned. That same year a small group left San Gabriel to found a new villa at Santa Fe. In 1610 a new governor, Don Pedro de Peralta, moved his capital to Santa Fe, establishing the first permanent European settlement in the American Southwest.

Although the Spanish presence there was limited, the impact on Native American life was dramatic. Residents of many pueblos were brought under Spanish control, and found that the Spanish were divided among themselves on how to approach colonization. Prominent colonists employed natives on their cattle ranches under grants of *encomienda*, and Spanish officials exploited Indian labor as allowed by *repartimiento*. Native labor was supposed to be paid, and the system was therefore seen as just in European terms, but for Indians who now left their native occupations and worked for wages, it was alienating. Moreover, settlers often ignored their obligation to recompense workers. Other Indians found themselves working on the fringes of Spanish communities. Those who remained in their pueblos were introduced to Spanish culture primarily through the priests who settled among them; these experienced a gentler, but still profoundly disorienting, process.

Pueblo life was also transformed by the activities of bands of Indians who increasingly raided their villages. Apaches and Navajos were themselves fairly recent arrivals in the Southwest; both were Athapaskan-speakers with roots in the far northern subarctic. As these bands had moved down across the continent, they had demonstrated marked adaptability to new environments. Now in the Southwest, the bands whom the Spanish labeled Apaches and Navajos once again adapted by designing new lifestyles around the Europeans' imported horses and sheep. Fugitive European animals had established herds in the American West long before settlement by European people. Harassed by slave-raiding expeditions against them from Spanish outposts, the highly mobile Athapaskans raided pueblos to gain captives to be traded for horses and equipment in northern Mexico. Pueblo-dwellers, who were committed to a sedentary life, were ill-equipped to resist such raids, and found themselves increasingly dependent on Spanish protection.[1]

Thus the small Spanish presence in the New Mexican territory dramatically changed life throughout the region, a transformation of which the newcomers themselves were only dimly aware.

V Quebec

WHILE THE ATTENTION OF GOVERNMENTS FOCUSED ON THE RUMORED riches of the South, fishermen from all over Europe continued to congregate in the North every summer. Demand for fish expanded with Europe's population, and the required investment remained low. Moreover, fishing could be carried out entirely by the efforts of the Europeans; they need not affect nor attempt to control the American natives. As Captain John Smith later pointed out, fishing, though unglamorous, brought great riches to those engaged in it: "Therefore honourable and worthy Country men, let not the meannesse of the word fish distaste you, for it will afford as good gold as the Mines of Guiana or Potassie [Potosí], with lesse hazard and charge, and more certainty and facility."[1]

The fur trade began as a spinoff from fishing; furs were brought back as a novelty by fishing parties. By the later sixteenth century the trade in furs became a major enterprise in its own right, routinely taking ships farther and farther into the Gulf of St. Lawrence. This new trade had immense and unforeseen consequences for native life, because the Europeans relied on Indian hunters and traders to carry it on. Whereas fishing had kept the newcomers on the coast in temporary shelters, the fur trade drew them inland. Coastal tribes, those that knew the Europeans and their ways best, now sought relationships with societies to the west who could furnish furs. And as natives increasingly specialized in providing furs for export, their economies became simplified and specialized, with consequent loss of skills relevant to their former range of economic activities. Thus they quickly became dependent on manufactured goods, especially metal tools and equipment from Europe.

Massive change along the St. Lawrence River during the second half of the sixteenth century speaks eloquently of the fur trade's effect. Cartier and Roberval had described a confederation of Iroquois settlements controlling the St. Lawrence in the 1530s and 1540s. When Samuel de Champlain retraced their route at the opening of the seventeenth century, he found few villages along the river; the St. Lawrence Iroquois, who had founded the great city of Hochelaga, had vanished. The new trade relationships favored mobility, the ability to range far into the interior, rather than settled urban life; Champlain and his men found nomadic, largely Algonquian, tribes had replaced the Iroquoians. Competition over control of the fur trade, and the flow of the much-desired European trade goods that fueled it, had brought sustained conflict and revolutionized native life.[2]

The fur trade also changed European attitudes toward settlement of the rugged region; the nation with a permanent presence would be able to forge exclusive relationships with the natives and dominate the enterprise. Late in the sixteenth century, new schemes for colonies in the North began to appear; the accumulated expertise of decades of fishing voyages made promoters confident they could overcome the problems that destroyed the Cartier-Roberval ventures. And the riches promised by the fur trade made the risks seem worthwhile. A series of small and poorly backed ventures set out in the 1580s and 1590s. Sir Humphrey Gilbert, Sir Walter Ralegh's older half-brother, made a voyage in 1583, an expedition that ended in his death. Troilus Mesgouëz, Sieur de la Roche, named Viceroy of Canada by the French king, gathered three hundred colonists to found a settlement in Newfoundland in 1584, but the ship ran aground. In 1597 a very small group of English separatist Protestants, an early example of the kind of religiously motivated plantation later successfully built by the Pilgrims in 1620, attempted to create a refuge on the Magdalen Islands at the mouth of the Gulf of St. Lawrence. That colony was driven off by a combined force of fishermen, fur traders, and Indians, all of whom saw settlement as a threat to the free and open trades.

Though we can see that poor planning was largely at fault, all these efforts reinforced the northern reputation as an inhospitable environment, a place where colonies failed. Nonetheless in 1598, just as Oñate renewed Spanish involvement in New Mexico, Sieur de la Roche again tried to create a reality to match his title of Viceroy of Canada, this time on Sable Island, ninety miles east of Nova Scotia. To aid him the French government rounded up eight hundred "strong tramps and beggars" in Rouen, from whom La Roche picked two hundred.[3] Experience had taught clearly that plantations required support, and La Roche faithfully sent supplies out in 1599, 1600, and 1601. In 1602, no ship sailed and the 1603 supply voyage found the colony almost completely deserted. The planters had mutinied, killed the governor and storekeeper, and vanished, never to be seen again. The remaining eleven colonists were evacuated back to France.[4]

A simultaneous venture under a French patent to Pierre Chauvin de Tonnetuit set out in 1600 to build a colony on the St. Lawrence River. This party chose unwisely to settle at Tadoussac ninety miles up the river, a location chosen for its trade position. Champlain later argued that the site had doomed the venture, "a place the most disagreeable and barren in the whole country . . . where the cold is so great that if there is an ounce of cold forty leagues up the river, there will be [a] pound of it here." Tadoussac survived as a small trading post, but never became the great center envisaged by Chauvin. Those who stayed suffered miserably during the winter.[5]

Thus at the opening of the seventeenth century the lessons of the North seemed clear, and they were not very different from the lore acquired much earlier: The region had rich resources in the form of fish and furs, but colonization was both far too difficult and too unpromising to be worth the effort. All this was soon to change.

French promoters continued to plan settlements. Samuel de Champlain first came to America in 1603, in a fleet sent to resupply Tadoussac, and explored up the St. Lawrence. Gains in linguistic understanding on both sides allowed him to conduct extensive interviews, and he came away with a sophisticated understanding of the way in which the great river connected with other waterways. He correctly interpreted information about the shape and extent of Hudson's Bay and the location of the Great Lakes, though he believed that the latter were salt water and thus hoped that accounts of Lake Huron actually described the Pacific. Champlain also realized that the fur trade was reaching deep into the interior, carrying French trade goods far beyond the ethnohistorical frontier.

Champlain returned with another expedition in 1604 that explored the coast of Nova Scotia and down the shore to Maine, noting good sites for plantations as they went. Eighty men remained for the winter in their new fort on Ste. Croix Island in Passamaquoddy Bay, a site chosen primarily for its defense capabilities but lacking in wood and water. The winter was miserable; the unprepared settlers had been misled by the latitude and expected winter to be no worse than in France. Scurvy took a terrible toll, and affected almost everyone. They knew that Annedda had cured Cartier's men, but found no knowledge of it among these natives. Champlain drew the lesson: "It is difficult to know this country without having wintered there; for on arriving in summer everything is very pleasant..." But, he went on, "There are six months of winter in that country."[6]

Despite the hardships the little colony carried on. In the spring, with fresh supplies from France, the explorers decided to explore farther south. Aided by maps drawn by the natives, Champlain explored Boston harbor and Cape Cod. But none of the places they saw appeared suitable for settlement. A second trip produced no more promising results. The Ste. Croix settlement was moved to Port Royal and suffered another discouraging winter.

Meanwhile English ventures also explored the New England coast, called Norembega at this time; they hoped to find and develop Verrazzano's "Refugio" (Newport Harbor). Voyages in 1602 and 1603 produced glowing reports of the region's possibilities. John Brereton, reporter of the 1602 voyage, praised the Indians' knowledge of the land as demonstrated by the maps they drew, and he indicated their sophisticated understanding of the dynamics of European trade. Brereton claimed that "the most fertil part of al England is (of it selfe) but barren" in comparison to New England. Brereton's *Briefe and True Relation of the Discoverie of the North Part of Virginia* included a treatise by Edward Hayes arguing "upon infallible reasons" that exploration would reveal "a way to be made part overland, & part by rivers or lakes into the South seas unto Cathay, China, and those passing rich countreys, lying in the East parts of the world," but "the same shall never be made knowen, unlesse we plant first; whereby we shall learne as much by inquisition of the naturall inhabitants, as by our owne navigations."[7] A third voyage, in 1605, produced another glowing and compelling account.

By 1607 then, despite many discouraging adventures, both France and England sustained a commitment to permanent settlement in the North. Champlain insisted that the failed colonies in Acadia should not doom French efforts; back in France after a three-year stay in America, he argued for a permanent settlement on "the great St. Lawrence river, which from my journey up it I knew well." Holding out the promise of finding the passage to the Pacific, he returned in 1608 at the head of a new colony. He chose Quebec as his site over the objections of his men who were frightened at the prospect of settling where so many of their countrymen had died; the remains of Cartier's fort were still visible. Champlain, drawing on his experience, put the men to work building a *habitacion,* with all the dwellings and storehouses in a square reachable from within a gallery around the outside.[8] Quebec, founded at the same time as the Spanish renewed their commitment to New Mexico, would defy the record of all previous French colonies and would survive to be the first permanent plantation in New France.

English settlement of the North did not fare so well. A settlement at Sagadahoc in Maine was sponsored in 1607 by a group of merchants centered in Plymouth, England. The winter of 1607-08 was exceptionally cold; the Thames froze solid that year. The little colony, lacking the sophisticated experience of Champlain and basing their planning on summer experience, folded in less than a year and the survivors returned home. Backer Sir Ferdinando Gorges lamented, "all our hopes were frozen to death."[9] As John Smith wrote a few years later when he tried to rehabilitate the region in

English eyes (he named it New England as part of this campaign), after the failure of Sagadahoc "the Country [was] esteemed as a cold, barren, mountainous, rocky Desart."[10] Twelve years later, however, English colonists would return to New England and this new plantation, that of the separatist Puritan Pilgrims at Plymouth, was designed on very different lines for new purposes.

VI Jamestown

ENGLISH PROMOTERS WERE ALSO INTERESTED IN THE SOUTH; AFTER the French and Spanish failure to settle the Carolina coast and Chesapeake Bay, English propagandists argued that God had reserved the heart of eastern North America for Protestant England. This contention found focus in a small group of influential men that formed around Sir Walter Ralegh. Geographer Richard Hakluyt wrote the famous "Discourse of Western Planting" to convince the queen and her ministers that only through American colonization could England become wealthy and powerful enough to take its place as a great nation alongside its rivals, Spain and France.[1] When Ralegh became a special favorite of Queen Elizabeth, he received riches and power sufficient to attempt to make the dream a reality. A reconnoitering voyage he sent out in 1584 reported that Roanoke Island, lying in the shallow sounds between the Carolina Outer Banks and the mainland—the "sea" that had misled Verrazzano—would be an ideal site for a colony that could also serve as a privateering base from which to attack the annual Spanish treasure fleet.

A full colony was sent out in 1585; this party of soldiers very quickly found that the site was quite poor. The island, like the Outer Banks, was composed mostly of sand and the waters around it were so shallow that ocean-going ships had to anchor out to sea. Thus its value as a base was illusory and the colonists were parasitic on the Indians; they lost most of their supplies when their main ship ran aground on landing at the treacherous banks. Indian relationships were transformed by the influx of European trade goods with which the men bought food; the neighboring Roanoke Indians became very powerful as the brokers through which other natives had access to the prized tools and beads. When the colonists' pressure became too great, the Roanokes resisted and Governor Ralph Lane of Roanoke, believing that their chief, Wingina, was using his newfound influence to assemble a military confederation to attack the settlement, launched what he conceived as a preemptive attack. After the fight, in which Wingina was killed, the dependent colonists could no longer count on Indian support. The soldiers gladly went home with Sir Francis Drake when he called in at Roanoke, hoping to use it as a base in the spring of 1586. Drake, in the tradition of the privateering war, had attacked and burned San Agustín as he sailed up the Florida coast.[2] Not surprisingly, the Spanish viewed the English, like the French, as mere lawless pirates.

The Roanoke colonists had spent the winter exploring. Lane led an expedition up the Chowan and Roanoke rivers searching for precious metals and the elusive route to the Pacific. He heard stories of wealthy people in a kingdom called Chaunis Temoatan, who lived on a great body of water to the west and had a gold-colored metal. These accounts were similar to those Cartier had earlier collected in the North. Cartier's Saguenay and Lane's Chaunis Temoatan may both have referred to Indians from the region of Lake Superior; their copper was spread by trade all over the eastern half of North America. Both men drew the hopeful conclusion that the metal might be gold, and the body of water the South Sea, the Pacific Ocean.

One solid accomplishment emerged from Lane's colony; while Lane explored the rivers, another party traveled overland to Chesapeake Bay and spent several months there. Reports of this area, notably the *Briefe and True Report of the New Found Land of*

Virginia written by Thomas Harriott, Sir Walter Ralegh's scientific advisor, convinced the backers that Chesapeake Bay offered the best site for further colonization.[3] Ralegh, acting on their information, determined to send a new set of planters to settle on the great bay, which could shelter the largest ocean-going ships. Not only was this colony to have a new destination, its composition was quite different. The new Roanoke colony was made up of families, each of whom was promised a substantial grant of land, and this was planned as a self-sustaining plantation.

The second Roanoke colony had hit upon both the location and the design that would ultimately bring success to English colonization, but satisfaction was denied to this venture. The planters, sent out in 1587, were deposited back at the inadequate Roanoke site for reasons that are not entirely clear. Governor John White, who had been with the earlier colony, blamed the expedition's pilot, a Portuguese named Simão Fernandes who had previously served the Spanish, for forcing the planters to remain there. Then Spain, increasingly harassed by the activities of marauders like Drake, determined to stop privateering once and for all. In 1588, King Philip II amassed the greatest fleet ever known to invade England, and the supply ships Ralegh had gathered to send to Roanoke were commandeered for England's defense. Not until 1590 did a relief ship reach Roanoke; by then the colonists were gone, leaving only the carved word CROATOAN on a post. Further attempts to search were frustrated, and these settlers became the famous Lost Colonists of Roanoke.

Some historians argue that the Roanoke colonists had made their way overland to Chesapeake Bay to settle in their intended location. Jamestown, the first permanent English colony, was planted on the James River very near their target site. Although they heard rumors of Europeans, the new settlers never saw any of the Lost Colonists.[4]

Jamestown's founding marked a new era in English enterprise. Queen Elizabeth died in 1603, ending a reign that spanned almost half a century. Her successor, James I, was intent on pursuing a peaceful policy. He brought the long conflict with Spain to an end and forbade the privateering that had fueled it. The merchant community, many of whom had become involved in American trades through privateering or fishing, now joined with gentlemen-courtiers in resolution to keep a permanent English presence there. Two great Virginia Companies were founded in 1606. One, centered in Plymouth, founded the short-lived Sagadahoc colony. The other, centered in London, planted Jamestown, basing their plans on information gathered by the Roanoke colonists. The London company differed from all previous English ventures in its large membership; the hundreds of investors meant that the company could ride out early difficulties and keep supplying the planters during the unproductive early years.[5]

Although the planners had learned much from earlier failures, the Virginia colony repeated many mistakes. Despite Ralph Lane of Roanoke's complaint that he could not control "ye wylde menn of myne owene nacione,"[6] early Jamestown contingents were composed entirely of soldiers and gentlemen, and the promoters had to learn the hard way that young men with military backgrounds were the least promising candidates either for building a new society or forging good relationships with the natives. The first winter was as devastating as Champlain's three years before at Ste. Croix Island in Passamaquoddy Bay, and the company dropped from just over one hundred to thirty-eight. But the English, like the French and Spanish, were now determined to maintain a foothold. Even another discouraging, starving winter in 1609-10 was not sufficient to deter the investors.[7] They resolved to deal with the problems of colonist control and direction by instituting a harsh regime of martial law under which the colony held on; like Santa Fe and Quebec, it contained little more than a token garrison for the next several years.

VII The Future of Colonization

COLONIZATION OF NORTH AMERICA WAS RETARDED; PERMANENT settlements, with the exception of San Agustín in Florida, were delayed until more than a century after colonization of the Caribbean and Central America. Interest in the region was high, but repeated attempts to establish a permanent presence were defeated. Europeans, for all their vaunted technology, fared badly in an environment in which American natives lived well.

The problems fell into two categories. The first was the sheer expense involved; staffing, sending, and sustaining a plantation ate up enormous amounts of money. Promoters who invested did so in the expectation of receiving greater revenues in return. When colonies were unable even to feed themselves, much less send back rich products, promoters lost interest. Many other trades beckoned to merchants, so there was little reason to continue a losing proposition. As Captain John Smith wrote, investors complained "that we feed You but with ifs and ands, hopes, and some few proofes."[1]

The other factor retarding interest in colonization was experience, which demonstrated that America did have valuable products, especially fish and furs, but that no expensive colonies were necessary to exploit them. Fishing and trading interests sometimes opposed settlers because they saw them as disrupting the relationships and assumptions on which the trades were based. In the South before the accession of James I the privateers found that they did not need a base like Roanoke; they were able to carry on without it.

Had understanding been better, European powers might not have gone ahead with creation of North American empires. Misconceptions, based on false fears and hopes, fed the drive to continue sending out parties. The Europeans remained convinced that a passage to the Pacific would be found and that the nation that controlled it would control the continent and the richest trade. Almost no amount of experience could kill this dream as long as any river system remained unexplored. It persisted into the nineteenth century, as can be seen in Jefferson's instructions to the Lewis and Clark expedition. The hope that gold or other precious minerals must exist also endured; writers constantly pointed out that the first peoples confronted by Columbus had little metal, but the Spanish found fabulous wealth as they moved west. The Virginia Company's instructions show the persistence of unrealistic hopes; they called for the colonists to find "the South Sea, a Mine of gold; or any of them sent by Sir Walter Ralegh [the Lost Colonists];" John Smith firmly told company officials nothing of the sort should be expected, but hopes lived on.[2]

Hope continued partly because exploratory expeditions always praised the land they had seen. That they would do so should have been foreseen. They wanted to assert the value of their own work; moreover many of them, seeing unfamiliar environments, must have been poorly equipped to judge how productive they might be. Their accounts take on a characteristic shape: Failure is explained by particular circumstances, or by the inadequacy of the men on whom the party was forced to rely. Circumstantial evidence of hidden riches is offered, along with reasons why it should be credited. The next venture, by implication, will overcome or avert problems and the promised rewards will be obtained. So stereotypical did these accounts become that skeptics in Europe began to dismiss all accounts. William Wood protested against "the unjust aspersion commonly laid on travailers; of whom many say, They may lye by authority."[3]

Overpraise set planners up for profound disappointment, as the harsh realities of North America were proven again and again. Not only was the environment rugged, with winters much more rigorous than knowledge of the same latitudes in Europe would have led them to expect, but rich commodities were scarce. The fish and furs they knew of did not require colonies, and nothing else seemed readily available.

Thus, in the first decade of the seventeenth century, North American European empires looked unlikely. Small outposts, established by hard-won experience, did exist but few would have predicted the massive influx of colonists that was soon to occur. What was required to make that happen was a complete overturning of previous notions of what colonies were to be for. Virtually all colonies to this point had been based on an extractive principle. European powers thought of them as adjuncts to the home country, and colonists, who were usually all young men, expected to be rotated home in time. Thus they all sought some commodity that could be extracted, preferably without much labor, or bought from the Indians and sent home to enrich both colonists and investors. The fur trade was the classic example of this kind of relationship.

In reality this strategy did not work well in North America. All commodities required development, and a human as well as a monetary investment. Not until Europeans began to think of America as a place to come and live out their lives, establishing homes to be passed on to their children, would these apparently unpromising lands be colonized. Colonists, willing and unwilling, would have to mix their labor with the land and produce the commodities to be sold in Europe. And these commodities would be much more humble products than the gold, jewels, or silk promoters envisioned. Virginia's economy took off when colonists began to cultivate tobacco; successes in other regions would come from similar products requiring labor and patience. The keys lay in learning about the environment and what it would grow, and then finding a commodity for which an infinitely expanding market existed or could be created in Europe.

France, Spain, and England each had a small North American settlement in existence by 1610. It was after 1620 that English commitment began to predominate. It is not accidental that the English came to dominate North America; they came in huge numbers in the first half of the seventeenth century and created the foundation for a large European population. In comparison, New France and the Spanish colonies north of the Rio Grande remained small. Spanish interest centered elsewhere, in their richer plantations to the south. French colonial development continued to focus on the fur trade; although French envoys ranged all over the interior of the continent, their numbers were limited. Since the fur trade involved a partnership with powerful Indian confederations able to command a position in the trade networks, the colonial authorities had no wish or need to displace natives with French farmers.

Only the English came to North America in large numbers in the 1620s and 1630s, the crucial decades for the founding of North American colonies. English men and women were willing to emigrate because conditions in England were very bad, with runaway inflation and a population explosion creating food shortages and a dramatic drop in real wages. Distress at home fed development abroad. Moreover, England was late in the race for colonies and had been frozen out of the more desirable areas. They came to develop the regions—the Chesapeake and New England—that other nations had elected not to attempt. And they came to set up farms and plantations on their own. English colonies offered land to virtually every prospective settler in the early years, offering a chance for stability and success that few could achieve at home.

All this added up to a very different conception of colonization. These settlements were not to be mere adjuncts to Europe, but were to attempt to replicate European society here. Although few or none understood the full implications of this shift in the 1630s, the crucial steps were taken during that decade, when tens of thousands emigrated in hopes of establishing economic independence for themselves and their families. Partly because of the English Civil War and its aftermath, which rent the nation during the period from 1640 to 1660, the colonists took much of their management into their own hands. In great part their success in establishing thriving economies stems from their taking direction of their own development. When, later in the century, the restored Stuart kings tried to impose control, they encountered great difficulty.

The development of North American colonies required a permanent commitment on the part of individual settlers to the land and the expectation of trade in colonist-produced commodities. It also required replication of something approaching normal European societies. Women were essential, as the secretary of the Virginia Assembly informed the Virginia Company in his report of the first meeting: "in a newe plantation it is not knowen whether man or woman be more necessary."[4] Once these principles were established, the settlers would spread over the land with a rapidity no one anticipated. And these farmers, taking over land and fencing in their rectangular plots to be held in perpetuity, threatened Indian life in ways far more fundamental than any soldier.

Within a decade, thousands of settlers joined the few hundred already on America's East Coast, on land formerly occupied exclusively by Indians. Neither European immigrants nor natives realized how fundamentally incompatible their land-use patterns were. The Indians combined intensive agriculture with hunting and gathering, and native lifeways required large amounts of land and abundance of species. Colonists' desire for land for themselves and their children, the magnet that drew them, required dividing up the land in plots and forbidding access by others. The European domesticated animals, set free to fend for themselves in the woods, competed for the nuts and berries the natives relied on. The most vulnerable varieties died out from the livestocks' repeated cropping, and the wild animals retreated from the frontier of settlement. Not only were the regions' wild food supplies hit, but the colonists' pigs rooted up the Indian cornfields and gardens, so natives were doubly impoverished. Humans and animals spread European diseases, which killed many Native Americans. In all these ways, the coming of the European agriculturalists despite, their avowedly peaceful intentions, wreaked far more havoc than the warlike soldiers.

ENDNOTES

Introduction

[1] Verrazzano to Francis I, July 8, 1524, in David B. Quinn, with Alison M. Quinn and Susan Hillier, eds., *New American World: A Documentary History of North America to 1612*, 5 vols. (New York, 1979), 1:281-88. This valuable collection brings together documents for all early ventures with a highly informative commentary and notes. Volume one also contains "Agreement made with Esteban Gómez, pilot, for the exploration of Eastern Cathay," 271-73, and excerpts of John Rut's letter to Henry VIII from Newfoundland, August 3, 1527, 189-90.

Chapter I: Northern Experience

[1] "Jacques Cartier's First Account of the New Land, Called New France, Discovered in the Year 1534," and "The second voyage undertaken by the command and wish of the Most Christian King of France, Francis the First of that name, for the completion of the discovery of the western lands . . . by Jacques Cartier, 1536," Quinn et al., *New American World*, 1:293-304, 304-28.

[2] On the Little Ice Age see Karen Ordahl Kupperman, "The Puzzle of the American Climate in the Early Colonial Period," *American Historical Review*, 87 (Dec. 1982), 1262-89.

[3] For contemporary understanding of scurvy see Karen Ordahl Kupperman, "Apathy and Death in Early Jamestown," *Journal of American History*, 66 (June 1979), 33-34.

[4] "The third voyage of discovery made by Captaine Jaques Cartier, 1540, unto the Countreys of Canada, Hochelaga, and Saguenay," ibid., 330-34; "The Voyage of John Francis de la Roche, knight, Lord of Roberval, to the Countries of Canada, Saguenai, and Hochelaga, . . . begun in April, 1542," in Quinn et al., *New American World*, 1:337-39.

[5] Richard Hakluyt, "The Voyage of master Hore and divers other Gentlemen, to Newfoundland, and Cape Breton, in the yeere 1536," in Quinn et al., *New American World,* 1:206-08.

[6] On the Newfoundland fishing industry see Harold A. Innis, *The Cod Fisheries: The History of an International Economy* (New Haven, 1940), ch. 2 and 3, and Gillian T. Cell, E*nglish Enterprise in Newfoundland, 1577-1660* (Toronto, 1969), ch. 1 and 2.

Chapter II: Southern Experience

[1] "True relation of the hardships suffered by Governor Don Fernando de Soto and certain Portuguese Gentlemen in the Discovery of the Province of Florida. Now newly set forth by a Gentleman of Elvas, 1557," in Quinn et al., *New American World,* 2:97-158. Other documents on Soto and his expedition are included, ibid., 90-96 and 159-88.

[2] "Narrative of the Expedition to Cíbola, Undertaken in 1540, in Which Are Described All Those Settlements, Ceremonies, and Customs. Written by Pedro de Castañeda of Náxera" in Quinn et al., *New American World,* 2:365-406, quote p. 373. Related documents are ibid., 406-32.

Chapter III: The View at Mid-Century

[1] René de Laudonnière told the story of these colonies in *L'histoire notable de la Floride,* 1586, published in English by Richard Hakluyt in 1587 and excerpted in Quinn et al., *New American World,* 2:294-307, 319-61. See his descriptions of the land's resources, pp. 281-82, 296-97, 339-40, 342. See also the excerpt from Lancelot Voisin, *Les Trois Mondes,* ibid., 307-08.

[2] On privateering see Kenneth R. Andrews, *Elizabethan Privateering* (Cambridge, 1964).

[3] Menéndez de Avilés to Philip II, October 15, 1565, in Quinn et al., *New American World,* 1:396-404; "Memorial Written by Doctor Gonzalo Solís de Merás of all the voyages and deeds of the Adelantado Pedro Menéndez de Avilés his brother-in-law and of the conquest of Florida and the justice he worked on Juan Ribao and the

other frenchmen," ibid., 424-55; Nicolas Le Challeux, *Discours de l'histoire de la Floride,* 1566, ibid., 370-79.

[4] Documents concerning this mission are collected in C. M. Loomis and A. J. Loomie, *The Spanish Jesuit Mission in Virginia, 1570-1572* (Chapel Hill, 1953). Further analysis of the confrontation occurs in Charlotte Gradie, "Spanish Jesuits in Virginia: The Mission that Failed," *Virginia Magazine of History and Biography,* 96 (1988), 131-56, and Carl Bridenbaugh, *Jamestown, 1544-1699* (New York, 1980), 10-19.

Chapter IV: Santa Fe

[1] On these events see Elizabeth A. H. John, *Storms Brewed in Other Men's Worlds: The Confrontation of Indians, Spanish, and French in the Southwest, 1540-1795* (College Station, Texas, 1975) ch. 1-2. On changes in Southwestern native life see ibid., and Edward H. Spicer, *Cycles of Conquest: The Impact of Spain, Mexico, and the United States on the Indians of the Southwest, 1533-1960* (Tucson, 1962), ch. 11; and Richard J. Perry, *Western Apache Heritage: People of the Mountain Corridor* (Austin, 1991), ch. 7-8.

Chapter V: Quebec

[1] Smith, *Generall Historie of Virginia, New-England, and the Summer Isles,* 1624, in Philip L. Barbour, ed., *The Complete Works of Captain John Smith (1580-1631),* 3 vols. (Chapel Hill, 1986), 2:474.

[2] For reconstruction of the Iroquoians' fate see Bruce G. Trigger, "Early Iroquoian Contacts with Europeans," in *Handbook of North American Indians,* vol. 15, Bruce G. Trigger, ed. (Washington, D.C., 1978), 346-47, and Trigger and James F. Pendergast, "Saint Lawrence Iroquoians," ibid., 357-61.

[3] "Order of the Parlement of Normandy, May 20, 1598" in Quinn et al., *New American World,* 4:309; Report of Monsieur Eaufranc, lieutenant general of the police of Rouen, ibid., 310.

[4] "Document sent by the Marquis Troïllus de Mesgouës de la Roche-Mesgouëz in Brittany to King Henry IV . . . chiefly on the subject of the trouble and opposition he met with in the Isle de Bourbon," 1606, in Quinn et al., *New American World,* 4:310-11.

[5] H. P. Biggar, gen. ed., *The Works of Samuel de Champlain*, 6 vols. (1922-36), 3:305-11.

[6] Champlain, *Voyages*, in Biggar, *Works of Champlain*, 1:204-469, quotes, 302-07.

[7] John Brereton, *A Briefe and True Relation of the Discoverie of the North Part of Virginia*, 1602, in David B. Quinn and Alison M. Quinn, eds., *The English New England Voyages, 1602-1608* (London, 1983), 143-203, quotes, pp. 152, 176-77.

[8] Champlain, *Voyages*, in Biggar, *Works of Champlain* 1:225-32; 2:3-156; 4:1-120, quote, 4:31.

[9] Sir Ferdinando Gorges, *A Briefe Relation of the Discovery and Plantation of New England*, 1622, in James Phinney Baxter, ed., *Sir Ferdinando Gorges and His Province of Maine*, 3 vols. (1890), 1:206-07. Gorges was a principal backer of the colony.

[10] Smith, *Generall Historie*, in Barbour, ed., *Complete Works*, 2:399.

Chapter VI: Jamestown

[1] E. G. R. Taylor, ed., *The Original Writings and Correspondence of the Two Richard Hakluyts*, 2 vols. (London, 1935), 2:211-326.

[2] All the documents associated with the Roanoke venture can be found in David Beers Quinn, ed., *The Roanoke Voyages, 1584-1590*, 2 vols. (London, 1955); many can also be found in Quinn et al., *New American World*, 3:265-340.

[3] Harriot, *Briefe and True Report of the New Found Land of Virginia* (orig. pub. 1588, 1590; repr. New York, 1972). Ralegh sent Harriott and the painter John White to produce a complete natural history of Virginia. This reprint edition included contemporary woodcuts of White's paintings. For an excellent modern, but limited, edition of the paintings themselves see Paul Hulton and D. B. Quinn, eds., *The American Drawings of John White, 1577-1590* (London, 1964). An inexpensive edition was printed for the Roanoke Quadricentenary; Paul Hulton, *America 1585: The Complete Drawings of John White* (Chapel Hill, 1984).

[4] See especially David Beers Quinn, S*et Fair for Roanoke: Voyages and Colonies, 1584-1606* (Chapel Hill, 1985), part IV.

[5] All the documents concerning Jamestown's founding are collected in Philip L. Barbour, ed., *The Jamestown Voyages Under the First Charter, 1606-1609*, 2 vols. (Cambridge, 1969).

[6] Ralph Lane to Sir Philip Sidney, 12 August 1585, in Quinn, ed., *Roanoke Voyages*, 1:204-06, quote, 204.

[7] For theories about the cause of the high death rate in Jamestown, see Karen Ordahl Kupperman, "Apathy and Death in Early Jamestown," *Journal of American History* 66 (June 1979), 24-40 and Carville V. Earle, "Environment, Disease, and Mortality in Early Virginia," in Thad W. Tate and David L. Ammerman, eds., *The Chesapeake in the Seventeenth Century: Essays on Anglo-American Society* (Chapel Hill, 1979), 96-125.

Chapter VII: The Future of Colonization

[1] *Generall Historie* in Barbour, ed., *Complete Works*, 2:187-88.

[2] Ibid.

[3] Wood, *New Englands Prospect* (London, 1634), sig. A3.

[4] John Pory, "A Reporte of the manner of proceeding in the general assembly convented at James City," in Susan Myra Kingsbury, ed., *The Records of the Virginia Company of London*, 4 vols. (Washington, D.C., 1906-35), 3:160.

SUGGESTIONS FOR FURTHER READING

Readers interested in pursuing this topic can read the many actual reports of the explorers and colonists that have survived to the present day. The reports provide a compelling view of the hopes that propelled the early voyagers and the difficulties they faced. The reports often also offer a great deal of information about the natives' response. Building on these reports, and aided by archaeology, modern scholars have illuminated these experiences. What follows is a brief guide to the literature.

The work of David Beers Quinn and Alison M. Quinn forms the basis for all scholarship on early exploration and colonization. David B. Quinn, *North America From Earliest Discovery to First Settlements: The Norse Voyages to 1612* (New York, 1975) is an excellent overview of the subject. All the relevant documents and excellent commentary are included in David B. Quinn, Alison M. Quinn, and Susan Hillier, eds., *New American World: A Documentary History of North America to 1612*, 5 vols. (New York, 1979).

For more information about Native Americans during the years of exploration and early colonization, two sources may be helpful. Bruce G. Trigger, ed., in *Handbook of North American Indians*, vol. 15 (Washington, D.C., 1978), includes valuable articles on Indians throughout the North American east, and on the impact of trade and colonization on native populations. This volume presents the fruits of recent scholarship and points to further sources on individual tribes and locales. Alvin M. Josephy, Jr., ed., in *America in 1492: The World of the Indian Peoples Before the Arrival of Columbus*, presents a rich discussion of Indian cultures and the life of the continent before the European intrusion. James Axtell offers an ethnohistorical perspective in his essays published as *After Columbus: Essays in the Ethnohistory of Colonial North America* (New York, 1988).

Paul E. Hoffman, *A New Andalucia and a Way to the Orient: The American Southeast During the Sixteenth Century* (Baton Rouge, 1990), and J. Leitch Wright, Jr., *Anglo-Spanish Rivalry in North*

America (Athens, Ga., 1971) discuss the international interest in the Southeast. The founding of Spanish Florida is treated in Eugene Lyon, *The Enterprise of Florida: Pedro Menéndez de Avilés and the Spanish Conquest of 1565-1568* (Gainesville, 1976), and Amy Turner Bushnell, *The King's Coffer: Proprietors of the Spanish Florida Treasury, 1565-1702* (Gainesville, 1981).

The story of the Roanoke colonies and the link to Jamestown's founding can be followed in David Beers Quinn, *Set Fair for Roanoke: Voyages and Colonies, 1584-1606* (Chapel Hill, 1985) and Karen Ordahl Kupperman, *Roanoke: The Abandoned Colony* (Totowa, N.J., 1984). Additionally, David B. Quinn and Alison M. Quinn have compiled an inexpensive collection of Roanoke sources, *The First Colonists: Documents on the Planting of the First English Settlements in North America, 1584-1590*, which is published by the North Carolina Dept. of Archives and History. Dover Books has printed a facsimile of Roanoke colonist Thomas Harriot's *Briefe and True Report of the New Found Land of Virginia* (1590) with sixteenth-century woodcuts. Jamestown's early years are treated in Alden Vaughan, *American Genesis: Captain John Smith and the Founding of Virginia* (Boston, 1975).

Two classic ethnohistorical studies of the complex relationships in the Southwest are Elizabeth A. H. John, *Storms Brewed in Other Men's Worlds: The Confrontation of Indians, Spanish, and French in the Southwest, 1540-1795* (College Station, Texas, 1975), and Edward H. Spicer, *Cycles of Conquest: The Impact of Spain, Mexico, and the United States on the Indians of the Southwest, 1533-1960* (Tucson, 1962). On the Athapaskans, see Richard J. Perry, *Western Apache Heritage: People of the Mountain Corridor* (Austin, 1991). Marc Simmons recounts the story of *The Last Conquistador: Juan de Oñate and the Settling of the Far Southwest* (Norman, Oklahoma, 1991), presenting events from the Spanish point of view. Simmons offers an excellent introduction to scholarship on the settlement of New Mexico.

On the earliest French settlement in the far north see Marcel Trudel, *The Beginnings of New France, 1524-1663*, trans. Patricia Claxton (Montreal, 1973). French-Indian contacts and their effects are the subject of Bruce G. Trigger, *Natives and Newcomers: Canada's "Heroic Age" Reconsidered* (Kingston and Montreal, 1985) and Olive Patricia Dickason, *The Myth of the Savage and the Beginnings of French Colonization in the Americas* (Edmonton, Alberta, 1984).

On New England prehistory see Neal Salisbury, *Manitou and Providence: Indians, Europeans and the Making of New England, 1500-1643* (New York, 1982). On the founding of the New England colonies, see Virginia DeJohn Anderson, *New England's Generation: The Great Migration and the Founding of Society and Culture in the Seventeenth Century* (Cambridge, 1991). For the colonists' sentiments see Everett Emerson, editor, *Letters from New England: The Massachusetts Bay Colony, 1629-1638* (Amherst, 1976).

For some of Captain Smith's writings on both Virginia and New England, see Karen Ordahl Kupperman, editor, *Captain John Smith: A Select Edition of His Writings* (Chapel Hill, 1988).